potatoes

potatoes

Annie Nichols

Photography by Peter Myers

RYLAND
PETERS
& SMALL

LONDON NEW YORK

Designer *Fiona Tweedie*
Commissioning Editor *Elsa Petersen-Schepelern*
Editor *Sharon Ashman*
Production *Patricia Harrington*
Art Director *Gabriella Le Grazie*
Publishing Director *Alison Starling*

Food Stylist *Annie Nichols*
Stylist *Wei Tang*

First published in Great Britain in 2003
by Ryland Peters & Small
Kirkman House
12–14 Whitfield Street
London W1T 2RP
www.rylandpeters.com

10 9 8 7 6 5 4 3 2 1

Printed in China

ISBN 1 84172 489 0

A CIP record for this book is available from the
British Library.

Recipes in this book have previously been
published in *Potatoes: from Gnocchi to Mash*
by Annie Nichols.

NOTES

All potatoes and other vegetables are washed then
peeled in the usual way, unless otherwise noted.

Where relevant, a particular type of potato is specified
in the recipes, such as floury or waxy. Where the type
of potato is not specified, use either variety.

Ovens should be preheated to the specified
temperature. If using a fan oven, cooking times should
be reduced according to manufacturer's instructions.

contents

DEDICATION

To Winnie and Fred Nichols, my Mum
and Dad, for a childhood full of
wholesome food, especially Dad's
new potatoes – the best in the west.

the basics

BOILING AND STEAMING POTATOES

New potatoes should be cooked in boiling salted water; old potatoes put in a saucepan of cold, lightly salted water then brought to the boil. Don't test for tenderness until towards the end of cooking time, or the potatoes will absorb water, become soggy and fall apart. Most of the nutrients are found just under the skin of the potato, so leave the skin on when boiling and peel them only when they are cooked. Peeled potatoes also absorb more water. Steaming takes a little longer than boiling. Boil or steam similar-sized potatoes together to make sure they cook evenly.

MASHING POTATOES

Soft, fluffy and creamy – mashed potato is the epitome of comfort food. It can be served as a side dish, as a dish in its own right, or used as the basis for many other recipes, such as croquettes or potato cakes. Potatoes cooked in their skins retain nutrients and have a dry texture, which absorbs liquids and flavourings better. If boiling peeled chunks of potato, drain when cooked, return to the saucepan, and let steam dry for a few minutes. Mash with a potato masher for a coarse texture, or press through a potato ricer or *mouli de legumes* for a fluffy, light texture. For an even lighter texture, heat liquids such as milk or cream before beating into the mashed potato.

Classic mashed potato recipe

Scrub 1 kg medium-sized floury potatoes, then boil in lightly salted water for 20–30 minutes until tender. Drain, cool and peel, then mash in 125 g butter. Reheat, season, then beat in 300 ml hot milk.

ROASTING POTATOES

The perfect roast potato has a crisp crunchy surface and soft, fluffy interior. Floury varieties are best for roasting, though small waxy ones, such as Pentland Javelin and Nadine, are also used in some cuisines, notably modern Italian. For extra flavour, roast potatoes with onions, garlic cloves in their skins, fresh thyme or rosemary. If potatoes are roasted with meat, the result will be less crisp, but they will have an excellent flavour.

Preparation

Potatoes can be roasted with or without the skins, but if peeled and cut into chunks, the pieces should be evenly sized so they cook at the same rate. Parboiling the potatoes first gives a soft interior and crisp edge. After parboiling, return the potatoes to the pan and shake them around the pan to roughen the edges slightly.

Oils and fats

The oil or fat used to roast potatoes is a matter of personal taste and regional tradition. Olive, sunflower or peanut oils are now the most common choices, largely for health reasons. However, duck and goose fat famously give the most wonderful flavour. Lard and dripping, now rarely used, also give a good flavour.

Roasting method, times and temperatures

Put oil or fat in a roasting tin large enough to hold the potatoes in a single layer, then heat in a preheated oven at 220°C (425°F) Gas 7. Add the potatoes to the hot oil (take care in case it splutters). Season with salt and pepper, then turn to coat with oil. Cook in the oven for 1 hour, turning occasionally, until crisp outside and tender inside. The time depends on the size of the potatoes.

DEEP-FRIED CHIPS

 Floury potato varieties, such as King Edward, Maincrops Maris Piper, Golden Wonder, Cara and Morene, are the best choice for chips. Use a deep-fryer or large, deep saucepan, and never use oil at a depth of more than a third to a half full. A wok, one- third full of oil, is also good. Always reheat oil to the required temperature between batches, and lower the potatoes gently into the oil to prevent splashing. A frying basket, wire scoop or slotted spoon lets you turn and lift the potatoes easily.

Do not overcrowd the pan, or the heat will be reduced and the potatoes boil rather than fry, absorb too much oil and become greasy and soggy.

Oils and fats

Peanut or corn oil cook at a high heat without burning. Olive oil is wonderful but extravagant. Sunflower oil, safflower oil and lard are also used. Always use clean oil, strain after use, and when reusing, remember what was cooked in it previously.

Frying method, times and temperatures

Perfect chips are twice-cooked. Cut the potatoes into long strips 5–15 mm thick, rinse well in cold water to remove the starch, then dry well. Fry in hot oil at 160°C (320°F) for 5 minutes until tender but pale, then drain well. Increase the heat to 190°C (375°F) and cook again for 1–2 minutes until crisp and golden. Check temperatures with a deep-frying thermometer or test-fry a cube of bread: it will turn golden in 1 minute at 180°C (350°F) or in 40 seconds at 190°C (375°F).

Safety first!

Always dry the potato well after rinsing, as excess water makes the oil splutter and boil. Never leave the pan unattended and clean up any spills immediately. Turn the handle of the pan away from the edge of the stove so it can't be knocked. If the oil starts to smoke, turn off the heat immediately. In the event of a fire, turn off the heat and cover the pan with a lid, baking sheet or a thick, damp cloth. Don't move the pan or use water to extinguish the fire. Let the pan cool completely before moving it.

soups, salads and snacks

potage parmentier

WITH PARSLEY OIL AND CROÛTONS

50 g unsalted butter

500 g floury potatoes, very
thinly sliced

1 onion, thinly sliced

1 bay leaf

900 ml milk

sea salt and freshly ground
black pepper

PARSLEY OIL

75 g fresh flat leaf parsley

125 ml extra virgin olive oil

CROÛTONS

3 tablespoons olive oil or
25 g unsalted butter

4 slices pancetta or
rindless streaky bacon

2 slices bread, crusts removed,
cut or broken into 1 cm pieces

SERVES 4

To make the parsley oil, bring a saucepan of water to the boil, add the parsley and blanch for 5–10 seconds. Drain and refresh in cold water. Drain well, then squeeze dry in a clean tea towel. Chop the parsley and put in a blender. Add the olive oil and purée until very smooth. Either leave it as it is, or strain the parsley oil first through a fine sieve, then again through 2 layers of muslin or a paper coffee filter. Pour into a clean bottle and use within 1 week.

To make the soup (potage), melt the butter in a large, heavy-based saucepan, add the potatoes and onion, stir and cover. Cook without colouring for 5–8 minutes, stirring occasionally, until the onion is softened and translucent.

Add the bay leaf, milk, salt and pepper and bring to the boil. Reduce the heat, cover and simmer for 15 minutes. Remove from the heat, discard the bay leaf, pour into a blender and purée until smooth. Strain through a very fine sieve into a clean pan.

To make the croûtons, heat the oil or melt the butter in a large frying pan over moderate heat. Add the pancetta or bacon and sauté for 5–6 minutes until crisp. Remove with a slotted spoon and drain on kitchen paper. Add the bread to the pan and cook, turning frequently, until crisp and golden. Drain on kitchen paper.

Reheat the soup, season with salt and pepper and serve sprinkled with parsley oil. Crumble the pancetta or bacon over the top, then add the croûtons, or serve them both separately.

potato mussel soup

WITH ITALIAN SUN-DRIED TOMATOES

a pinch of saffron strands

125 ml boiling water

175 ml dry white wine

1 kg mussels, scrubbed, debearded, broken or open ones discarded

fish or chicken stock (see method)

2 tablespoons olive oil

1 onion, sliced

1–2 garlic cloves, crushed

3 cm fresh ginger, peeled and finely grated

500 g potatoes, cut into 3 cm cubes

250 g tomatoes, skinned and chopped

8–10 sun-dried tomatoes, finely chopped

grated zest and juice of 1 unwaxed orange

a sprig of thyme

sea salt and freshly ground black pepper

fresh flat leaf parsley, chopped, to serve

SERVES 4

Put the saffron in a small heatproof bowl, pour over the boiling water and let infuse. Pour the white wine into a saucepan large enough to hold all the mussels. Bring to the boil, add the mussels, cover with a tight-fitting lid and cook, shaking the pan frequently, for 2–3 minutes until the mussels have opened.

Tip the mussels into a colander set over a bowl to catch the juices and discard any mussels that have not opened. Remove two-thirds of the mussels from their shells, discard the empty shells and set all the mussels aside. Strain the mussel liquid through a muslin-lined sieve or coffee filter paper into a jug. Measure the liquid and make up to 900 ml with fish or chicken stock or water. Set aside.

Heat the olive oil in a large saucepan, add the onion, garlic and ginger and cook for 5–10 minutes until the onion is softened and translucent. Add the potatoes, tomatoes, sun-dried tomatoes and orange zest and cook for 1–2 minutes more. Add the reserved stock, thyme, saffron and saffron soaking liquid, bring to the boil, reduce the heat, then simmer for 15 minutes until the potatoes are tender.

Add the orange juice and all of the mussels. Reheat, season with salt and pepper and serve sprinkled with the chopped parsley.

Many Australians with European roots still follow the cooking traditions of their country of origin. This Australian dish is a fine example of how the ingredients of one culture are absorbed into another.

Though creamy mayonnaise-style sauces are the traditional dressings for cold potato salads, highly flavoured dressings based on extra virgin olive oil have become popular with modern chefs.

roasted warm potato salad

1 kg small new or salad potatoes, unpeeled and scrubbed

125 ml extra virgin olive oil

1 small red onion, finely chopped

25 g pitted black olives, finely chopped

1½ tablespoons capers, rinsed and drained

6 sun-dried tomatoes in oil, drained and chopped

5 tablespoons chopped fresh flat leaf parsley

1 tablespoon balsamic vinegar

sea salt and freshly ground black pepper

SERVES 4–6

Put the potatoes in a roasting tin, add 2 tablespoons olive oil, sprinkle with salt and toss well to coat. Cook in a preheated oven at 200°C (400°F) Gas 6 for 25–30 minutes, or until tender, turning the potatoes from time to time.

Meanwhile, put all the remaining ingredients in a large bowl, mix well and season with salt and pepper.

Remove the potatoes from the oven, crush each potato slightly with a fork and cut in half. Toss the potatoes well in the bowl of dressing while they are still warm. Serve either warm or cold.

This Saudi Arabian salad combines a traditional Middle Eastern ingredient, the chickpea, with the more recent arrival, the potato. Both are particularly good at absorbing spicy flavours.

sultan's salad

125 g dried chickpeas

1–2 garlic cloves, chopped

50 g shelled walnuts

4 tablespoons chopped fresh
flat leaf parsley

2 tablespoons chopped fresh mint

4 tablespoons tahini paste

4–5 tablespoons freshly squeezed
lemon juice

75 ml extra virgin olive oil

about 75 ml water

a pinch of paprika

750 g new or waxy potatoes,
unpeeled and scrubbed

sea salt

TO SERVE (OPTIONAL)

2 tablespoons chopped walnuts

1 tablespoon toasted sesame seeds

4 sprigs of mint

SERVES 4

Put the chickpeas in a large bowl, cover with cold water and let soak overnight.

The next day, drain the chickpeas and rinse well. Put in a saucepan of cold water (do not add salt as this will make the chickpeas tough), bring to the boil, reduce the heat and simmer for 50 minutes to 1 hour or until tender. Drain well and reserve in a large bowl.

Put the garlic, walnuts and herbs in the bowl of a food processor or blender. Blend until finely chopped. Add the tahini paste and 4 tablespoons lemon juice and blend to mix. With the motor running, add the olive oil in a steady stream until amalgamated. Add enough water to make a thin dressing. Pour the dressing into a bowl and season with salt, paprika and more lemon juice if needed.

Bring a saucepan of lightly salted water to the boil, add the potatoes and simmer for 15–20 minutes or until tender. Drain well, then cut the potatoes in half and add to the chickpeas.

Pour over the dressing and toss well while still warm. Serve warm or at room temperature, sprinkled with chopped walnuts, toasted sesame seeds and fresh mint sprigs, if using.

empanaditas

To make the spicy potato filling, bring a saucepan of lightly salted water to the boil, add the potatoes and parboil for 2–3 minutes, drain well and let cool. Put the remaining filling ingredients in a bowl and mix. Stir in the cooled potatoes and season with salt and pepper.

Sieve the flour and salt into a large bowl, stir in the butter and add enough water to form a soft but firm dough. Knead briefly, wrap in clingfilm and let rest for 30 minutes at room temperature.

Roll out the dough on a lightly floured surface to about 3 mm thick. Using the saucer as a template, cut out 16 circles of 12 cm diameter. Knead and re-roll any trimmings. Put 1 tablespoon filling on each round, a little off-centre.

Dampen the edges of the pastry with a little water and fold in half over the filling. Using the prongs of a fork, press the edges together to seal them. Put the empanaditas on a tray and refrigerate for 30 minutes to 1 hour.

Heat the oil in a deep pan to 190°C (375°F) or until a cube of bread browns in 40 seconds. Fry the empanaditas in batches, turning once, for 3–5 minutes, or until golden brown. Drain on kitchen paper and serve, accompanied by a spicy fruit salsa, if using.

250 g plain flour

½ teaspoon salt

100 g butter, melted

2–2½ tablespoons water

sunflower oil, for deep-frying

spicy fruit salsa, to serve (optional)

SPICY POTATO FILLING

2 potatoes, cut into 5 mm cubes

3 spring onions, chopped

125 g canned sweetcorn kernels, drained

1–2 green chillies, deseeded and finely chopped (optional)

75 g ricotta or goats' cheese, crumbled

1 tablespoon chopped fresh marjoram

½ teaspoon paprika

sea salt and freshly ground black pepper

a saucer, 12 cm diameter

MAKES 16

Empanaditas are tiny turnovers popular in Spain and Latin America. They usually have savoury fillings, as here, but they can be filled with fruit and served as a pudding.

750 g large floury potatoes

2 fresh green chillies,
deseeded and finely chopped

½ teaspoon crushed dried red chillies

1 small onion, finely chopped

1 teaspoon sea salt

1 teaspoon ground cumin

1 teaspoon ground turmeric

2 tablespoons chopped fresh
coriander leaves

25 g unsalted butter, melted

150 g plain flour

sunflower oil, for frying

COCONUT AND MINT CHUTNEY

125 g grated fresh coconut or
75 g unsweetened desiccated coconut

200 g plain yoghurt

1 fresh green chilli, deseeded
and chopped

2 tablespoons chopped fresh mint

½ teaspoon salt

½ teaspoon sugar

MAKES 64

India has dozens of different kinds of bread – plain, with spicy fillings or flavoured with spices, as here. They are usually served with curry or dhaal, but these roti are made smaller to be eaten as a snack.

mini potato roti
WITH COCONUT AND MINT CHUTNEY

If using desiccated coconut to make the chutney, put it in a bowl and cover with warm water. Let soak for 20 minutes, then strain through a sieve, pressing the coconut against the sides of the sieve to squeeze out any excess moisture. Put all the chutney ingredients in a bowl, mix well and set aside.

Put the potatoes in a large saucepan of lightly salted water and bring to the boil. Simmer for 20–30 minutes or until tender. Drain and mash well. Add all the remaining ingredients, except the flour and oil, to the potatoes and mix well. Gradually mix in the flour until you have a soft dough. Divide the dough into 64 equal-sized pieces. Taking one piece at a time roll out on a floured board to approximately a 7 cm circle. Continue with the remaining pieces of dough.

Heat a little oil in a heavy-based frying pan and cook the roti 2 or 3 at a time for 1–2 minutes on each side until lightly browned. Serve with the coconut and mint chutney.

pizza con le patate

PIZZA DOUGH

15 g fresh yeast, 1 tablespoon dried active yeast or 1 sachet easy-blend dried yeast

a pinch of sugar

200 ml warm water

375 g strong white bread flour, plus extra for sprinkling

2 tablespoons olive oil

½ teaspoon salt

HERBY POTATO TOPPING

500 g waxy potatoes, thinly sliced

2 tablespoons extra virgin olive oil

4 garlic cloves, crushed

leaves from 2 sprigs of rosemary

1 teaspoon sea salt flakes

2 baking sheets

MAKES 2 PIZZAS, 23–25 CM DIAMETER

To make the pizza dough, put the fresh yeast, if using, and sugar in a small bowl and blend well. Mix in the warm water and leave for 10 minutes or until frothy. For other yeasts follow the instructions on the packet.

Sieve the flour into a large bowl and make a well in the centre. Pour in the yeast mixture, olive oil and salt. Mix to form a soft but firm dough. Turn out on to a lightly floured surface and knead the dough for 10 minutes until smooth.

Divide the dough in half and form into 2 balls. Put the dough balls on a lightly floured surface or tray in a warm place and sprinkle them liberally with flour. (This will become the base of each pizza and make it easier to slide on to the baking sheet.) Let rise for about 1 hour or until doubled in size.

Put the baking sheets in a preheated oven at 220°C (425°F) Gas 7 until hot. Put the potato slices, olive oil, garlic, rosemary and salt in a large bowl and stir to coat the potato.

Brush off any excess flour from the top of the dough, then turn the balls out on to a work surface and roll and pull each one out to a large circle, about 23–25 cm diameter. Spread the potato mixture evenly over both pizzas. Remove the sheets from the oven and slide 1 pizza on to each one. Sprinkle with more olive oil and salt if required, then bake for 15–20 minutes until the potatoes are tender and the pizza bases lightly golden and crisp.

This is the Italian takeaway snack, *pizza al trancio*, usually found in bakeries where slices are heated up for you (*trancio* means 'slice').

I discovered this delicious tart in New Mexico. The chilli kick is quite subtle – roasting them softens their flavour. Potatoes are great partners for the verve of chilli, and you can also add chilli to the pastry for more zest.

chilli potato tart

WITH ROASTED TOMATOES AND GARLIC

3 tablespoons extra virgin olive oil

750 g ripe red plum tomatoes, halved lengthways, then deseeded

4 whole garlic cloves, unpeeled

1 large red chilli

1½ teaspoons sea salt flakes

1 tablespoon caster sugar

500 g waxy potatoes, boiled in their skins for 15 minutes, then peeled and thinly sliced

300 ml crème fraîche, lightly whipped and seasoned with salt and pepper

sea salt and freshly ground black pepper

PASTRY

200 g plain flour

a pinch of salt

100 g unsalted butter

25 g finely grated Parmesan cheese

1 red chilli, deseeded and very finely chopped (optional)

a baking sheet

a tart tin, 25 cm diameter, greased

baking beans

SERVES 6

To roast the tomatoes, lightly brush a baking sheet with some of the olive oil and add the tomatoes, cut side up. Add the garlic and whole chilli and sprinkle the tomatoes evenly with the remaining olive oil, salt and sugar. Cook in a preheated oven at 180°C (350°F) Gas 4.

Remove the garlic from the oven after 10–15 minutes when soft and squeeze the flesh into a bowl. Remove the chilli after 15–20 minutes when the skin is blistered and slightly charred. Leave the tomatoes for 45–50 minutes until very soft and slightly charred. Let the chilli cool a little, then peel, deseed and finely chop. Add to the garlic. Scoop the tomato flesh out of the skins, add to the garlic, then mash with a fork and season with salt and pepper.

To make the pastry, sieve the flour and salt into a bowl. Rub in the butter using your fingertips until the mixture resembles breadcrumbs. Stir in the Parmesan and chilli, if using. Add enough cold water to make a firm dough, then roll out on a lightly floured surface and use to line the greased tart tin. Lightly prick the base all over with a fork. Chill for 30 minutes, then line with foil and baking beans. Heat a baking sheet on the middle shelf of a preheated oven at 200°C (400°F) Gas 6. Put the tart shell on the sheet, bake for 10–15 minutes, then remove the foil and beans.

Increase the oven temperature to 230°C (450°F) Gas 8. Spread the tomato mixture evenly over the tart base, then arrange the potato slices in concentric circles over the top. Pour the crème fraîche over the potato and bake for 8–10 minutes until the top is lightly golden.

meat and poultry

straw potato pancakes

WITH BARBECUED DUCK BREASTS

Scoop out the pomegranate seeds, discarding the white pith. Reserve 3 tablespoons seeds, cover and chill. To make the marinade, put the remaining seeds in a blender and process briefly to release the juice.

Strain through a fine sieve into a shallow, non-metallic dish. Add the lemon zest, garlic and ginger and stir. Add the duck to the marinade, turn to coat, cover and chill for 12–24 hours, turning occasionally.

Cut the potatoes into thin julienne strips using a mandolin or sharp knife, and rinse in cold water. Drain and rinse the potatoes 2–3 times to remove the starch. Drain, then dry well on a clean tea towel. Put in a bowl and season well with salt and pepper.

Heat the butter and oil in a large frying pan. Add spoonfuls of the potato to make 4 cakes. Press down slightly with the back of the spoon and cook for 8–10 minutes. Turn over and cook for 5–6 minutes more. Remove from the pan and keep them warm in a low oven.

Remove the duck from the marinade, reserving the marinade. Pat the duck dry and put on a preheated stove-top grill pan or barbecue. Cook, skin side down, for 5 minutes, then turn and cook for 5 minutes more until tender, but still pink. Let rest for 5 minutes, then slice thinly.

Put the marinade and honey in a small saucepan, bring to the boil and reduce until thickened. Season to taste with salt and pepper. To serve, put the pancakes on 4 warmed plates, top with the duck slices and reserved pomegranate seeds. Pour over the reduced marinade and sprinkle with chopped hazelnuts and salad leaves.

3 pomegranates, halved

zest of 1 preserved lemon, chopped

1 garlic clove, crushed

3 cm piece of fresh ginger, peeled and finely grated

4 small duck breasts, skin scored 3–4 times

500 g waxy potatoes

2 tablespoons clarified butter, plus extra if needed (see page 56)

1 tablespoon hazelnut oil

2 tablespoons honey

50 g roasted hazelnuts, chopped

a few salad leaves

sea salt and freshly ground black pepper

SERVES 4

This is a wonderful yellow-orange stew, heavily scented with the spices of the Middle East.

chicken potato stew

WITH SEVILLE ORANGES

a large pinch of saffron strands

2 tablespoons olive oil

1 whole chicken, about 2 kg,
cut into 8 pieces

2 tablespoons plain flour

1 teaspoon salt, plus extra to taste

crushed black seeds from 6 green
cardamom pods

1 teaspoon whole cloves

1 teaspoon allspice berries

1 teaspoon whole black peppercorns

1 teaspoon whole pink peppercorns

2 cinnamon sticks, 7 cm each

freshly squeezed juice of 2 oranges

freshly squeezed juice of 2 lemons

750 g floury potatoes, cut into
7 cm chunks

1 unwaxed lemon, sliced

1 unwaxed orange, sliced

1–2 tablespoons rosewater

steamed rice, to serve (optional)

SERVES 4

Put the saffron strands in a small heatproof bowl and pour over boiling water to cover. Set aside to infuse.

Heat the olive oil in a large casserole and fry the chicken pieces to seal them, 2 or 3 pieces at a time, until lightly golden all over. Transfer the chicken to a plate. Drain off all but 1 tablespoon of the fat from the casserole. Add the flour and cook for 1–2 minutes, then add the saffron and its infusing water. Stir well.

Return the chicken pieces to the casserole, add the salt, spices, orange and lemon juice. Pour over enough water to cover (about 1.2 litres), and bring to the boil.

Add the potatoes and orange and lemon slices. Reduce the heat to low, cover with a lid and simmer gently for 30 minutes or until the potatoes are tender, occasionally skimming off any fat that rises to the surface.

Taste and season with salt and pepper, then stir in rosewater to taste. Serve with steamed rice, if using.

When mixed with wheat flour, or even made into potato flour, potatoes give a wonderful texture to baked goods. Pastry made with potato, for instance, is light and crumbly.

1 kg floury potatoes, cut into
even-sized pieces

50 g unsalted butter

1 egg, beaten

150 g self-raising flour

1 teaspoon caraway seeds

sea salt and freshly ground
black pepper

CHICKEN LIVER FILLING

50 g unsalted butter

1 onion, finely chopped

1 celery stalk, finely chopped

1 carrot, finely chopped

500 g chicken livers, trimmed

½ teaspoon paprika

1 tablespoon tomato purée

125 ml white wine or chicken stock

4 tablespoons chopped fresh parsley

sea salt and freshly ground
black pepper

TO COAT

1 egg, beaten

50 g fine dry breadcrumbs

a saucer, 12 cm diameter

a baking sheet, greased

MAKES 16–18

potato turnovers

WITH CHICKEN LIVERS

Put the potatoes in a large saucepan of lightly salted water and
bring to the boil. Simmer for 20–30 minutes or until soft. When cool
enough to handle but still warm, peel the potatoes and pass through
a potato ricer or mouli, or push through a sieve into a large bowl.
Add the butter, egg, salt and pepper to the potato and beat well.
Gradually knead in the flour and caraway seeds until well mixed.
Turn on to a lightly floured surface and roll out to about 5 mm thick.
Let cool completely.

To make the filling, melt the butter in a frying pan. Add the onion,
celery and carrot and cook for about 5 minutes, until softened and
lightly golden. Increase the heat, add the chicken livers and cook,
stirring frequently, until sealed all over, about 5 minutes. Stir in the
paprika, tomato purée, wine or stock and chopped parsley. Season
with salt and pepper and let cool.

Using the saucer as a template, cut the potato dough into circles
of 12 cm diameter. Put 1 tablespoon filling on each circle, a little
off-centre. Fold the dough over the filling and press the edges
together firmly. Put on the greased baking sheet, brush with some
beaten egg, sprinkle with breadcrumbs and cook in a preheated
oven at 200°C (400°F) Gas 6 for 20–30 minutes until golden. Serve
as a snack or a light lunch with salad.

2 tablespoons sunflower oil

750 g boneless chicken (breasts or thighs), cut into large chunks

2–3 tablespoons red or green Thai curry paste

600 ml canned coconut milk

2½ tablespoons Thai fish sauce (*nam pla*)

2 tablespoons light brown sugar

500 g new potatoes, unpeeled, scrubbed and cut in half

½ teaspoon salt

1–2 tablespoons freshly squeezed lime juice

TO SERVE

50 g unsalted roasted peanuts

3 spring onions, cut into fine shreds and put in a bowl of cold water

Thai basil or coriander, chopped

2 kaffir lime leaves, thinly sliced (optional)

steamed jasmine rice

SERVES 4

A very simple, delicious curry with all the flavours of Thailand. Fish sauce (*nam pla*) and Thai curry pastes are available in large supermarkets and Southeast Asian stores.

thai chicken curry

WITH POTATOES AND COCONUT MILK

Heat the oil in a large wok or frying pan, add the chicken pieces, in batches if necessary, and fry them briefly on all sides to seal. Transfer the chicken pieces to a bowl.

Add the curry paste to the pan and stir-fry for about 30 seconds to release the aromas of the chillies and spices. Add the coconut milk, fish sauce and sugar and stir well. Return the sautéed chicken to the pan, together with any juices that have accumulated in the bowl.

Bring the mixture to the boil, then add the potatoes and salt. Reduce the heat, cover the pan and simmer for 15–20 minutes until the chicken is cooked and the potatoes are tender.

Stir in the lime juice to taste and more salt, if needed. Serve sprinkled with the peanuts, drained spring onion strips, basil or coriander and the kaffir lime leaf strips, if using. Steamed jasmine rice is an authentic accompaniment.

potato-crust lamb

WITH POACHED TAMARILLOS

750 g waxy potatoes

1 garlic clove, crushed

2 tablespoons chopped fresh chives

2 tablespoons chopped fresh
flat leaf parsley

1 tablespoon fresh thyme leaves,
removed from stalk

2 large egg yolks, beaten

12 lamb cutlets, very well trimmed,
with all fat removed and the bone
scraped clean

3 tablespoons olive oil

sea salt and freshly ground
black pepper

sprigs of thyme, to serve

POACHED TAMARILLOS

6 tamarillos

150 ml port or red wine

150 ml chicken stock

3 tablespoons honey

5 cm cinnamon stick

½ teaspoon crushed coriander seeds

a strip of unwaxed orange zest

SERVES 4

Grate the potatoes finely and do not rinse. Wrap in a clean tea towel and squeeze well to extract any excess liquid. Put the grated potato in a bowl and add the garlic, herbs and egg yolks. Season with salt and pepper and mix well. Divide into 12 parts and wrap each lamb cutlet completely with a portion of the mixture.

To prepare the tamarillos, cut a small cross at the pointed end of each one with a sharp knife. Bring a saucepan of water to the boil, add the tamarillos and blanch for 30 seconds. Lift out with a slotted spoon and plunge into cold water.

To make the sauce, carefully peel all the tamarillos, and finely chop 2 of them. Put the chopped tamarillos in a shallow saucepan, then add the port or red wine, stock, honey, cinnamon, crushed coriander seeds and orange zest. Bring to the boil, reduce the heat, add the whole tamarillos and simmer for 3–4 minutes. Lift the whole fruit out of the sauce and set aside. Increase the heat and boil the sauce rapidly for 2–3 minutes or until well reduced.

Heat the oil over moderate heat in 2 large heavy-based frying pans. Add the lamb cutlets and cook for 3–4 minutes on each side or until the potato is cooked and crispy and the lamb still pink. Slice the tamarillos but leave them attached at the stalk, then return them to the sauce and reheat gently.

To serve, put 3 cutlets and 1 sliced tamarillo on each plate. Spoon over a little sauce and sprinkle with thyme sprigs.

Tamarillos are a sub-tropical fruit. They can be bought in large supermarkets, but if unavailable, use plums or apricots instead.

These little fried cakes of potato and chorizo with a crisp corn salsa are based on a dish I discovered in Mexico.

750 g potatoes, unpeeled and well scrubbed

3 chorizo sausages, 80 g each, peeled and crumbled

1 garlic clove, crushed

4 spring onions, chopped

250 g goats' cheese, crumbled

1 egg, beaten

75 g fine dry breadcrumbs

olive oil, for frying

salad leaves, to serve

sea salt and freshly ground black pepper

CORN SALSA VERDE

1 tablespoon Dijon mustard

1 tablespoon freshly squeezed lime juice or wine vinegar

150 ml extra virgin olive oil

2 tablespoons capers, rinsed, drained and chopped

75 g canned sweetcorn kernels, drained

2 spring onions, finely chopped

1–2 garlic cloves, finely chopped

6 tablespoons chopped fresh flat leaf parsley

6 tablespoons chopped fresh coriander

1–2 green chillies, finely chopped

sea salt and freshly ground black pepper

SERVES 6

tortitas de papa

WITH CHORIZO AND CORN SALSA VERDE

Put the potatoes in a large saucepan of lightly salted water and bring to the boil. Simmer for 20–30 minutes or until tender. Drain well and when cool enough to handle, peel and pass through a potato ricer or mouli, or push through a sieve into a large bowl.

Heat a non-stick frying pan, add the chorizo and sauté gently for 5–10 minutes until the fat renders. Remove the chorizo with a slotted spoon, let cool slightly, then add to the potato. Add the garlic, spring onions and goats' cheese to the potato mixture and mix well. Add the egg, then season with salt and pepper and stir well.

Divide the mixture into 18 parts and make into small flat cakes. Roll each one in the breadcrumbs, pressing gently so the crumbs stick. Set aside while you make the salsa verde.

To make the salsa verde, put the mustard in a small bowl and whisk in the lime juice or wine vinegar. Continue whisking, adding the olive oil in a thin stream until amalgamated. Stir in the remaining salsa ingredients, then season with salt and pepper to taste.

Heat the olive oil in a large non-stick frying pan and fry the potato cakes in batches until golden brown all over (8–10 minutes). Drain on kitchen paper. Keep them warm while you cook the remaining cakes.

Serve with the salsa verde and crisp salad leaves, such as the mizuna, rocket and baby spinach shown here.

one-dish meals

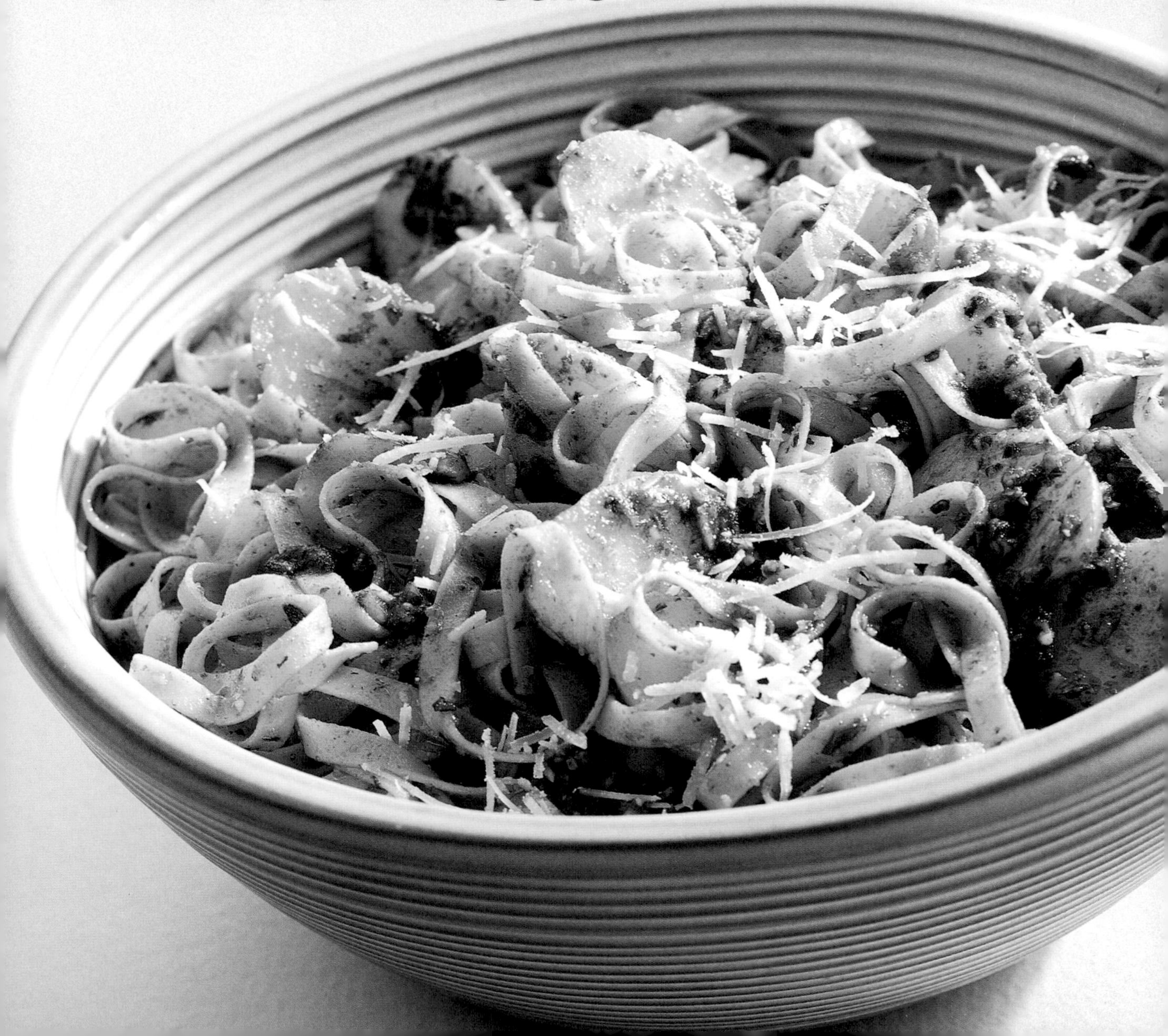

This combination of pasta and potatoes comes from an Italian-Australian friend of mine. Though not traditionally Italian, this dish is characteristic of the 'fusion food' found in Australia.

pasta and potatoes

WITH MACADAMIA PESTO

500 g new or salad potatoes, unpeeled and scrubbed

500 g tagliatelle

MACADAMIA PESTO

50 g fresh basil

75 g unsalted macadamia nuts, chopped

2 garlic cloves, chopped

175 ml extra virgin olive oil

50 g Parmesan cheese, finely grated, plus extra to serve (optional)

sea salt and freshly ground black pepper

SERVES 4

To make the pesto, put the basil, macadamia nuts and garlic in a blender or food processor and process until finely chopped. With the motor running, gradually add the oil in a thin stream until amalgamated. Scrape into a bowl, stir in the Parmesan and season to taste with salt and pepper.

Bring a saucepan of lightly salted water to the boil, add the potatoes and cook for 10–15 minutes, or until just tender. Drain and let cool slightly, then peel and cut into 5 mm slices.

Cook the pasta in a large saucepan of lightly salted boiling water, according to the packet instructions. Drain in a colander but leave 2–3 tablespoons of the cooking water in the bottom of the pan. (A small amount of cooking water will help the sauce to amalgamate and cling to the pasta.)

Return the pasta to the pan, add the potato slices and half of the pesto and mix well. (Refrigerate the remaining pesto to use in another dish.) Taste and season with salt and pepper. Serve immediately, sprinkled with extra Parmesan, if using.

This recipe is based on a Persian potato omelette but with broad beans added. Use frozen broad beans if you can't find fresh ones.

kuku sibzamini

250 g broad beans, podded if fresh, defrosted if frozen

500 g cooked potatoes, mashed

6 eggs, beaten

1 teaspoon ground turmeric

6 spring onions, chopped

2 tablespoons chopped fresh coriander

1 tablespoon chopped fresh flat leaf parsley

25 g unsalted butter

sea salt and freshly ground black pepper

SERVES 6–8

If using fresh broad beans, blanch them in lightly salted boiling water for 4 minutes, then drain. Refresh in cold water, then drain again. Pop the fresh or defrosted broad beans out of their skins, set aside, discarding the skins.

Put the mashed potato in a large bowl, then stir in the beaten eggs and ground turmeric. Fold in the broad beans, spring onions and herbs, then season with salt and pepper.

Put the butter in a heavy-based non-stick frying pan with a heatproof handle, and melt over moderate heat. Pour in the potato mixture. Reduce the heat to very low and cook without stirring for 15–20 minutes or until the eggs have set and the base is golden brown (check by lifting the edge of the omelette with a palette knife).

Put the pan under a preheated grill to brown the top of the omelette, then slide it on to a large plate or tray and cut into small squares or wedges. Serve hot or cold.

The success of gnocchi depends on lightly
mixing the potato and flour to the right
consistency – smooth and slightly sticky.
If you over-mix, the gnocchi will be heavy.

potato gnocchi

WITH WALNUT AND ROCKET PESTO

To make the pesto, put the rocket, walnuts and garlic in a blender or food processor and process until finely chopped. Add the olive oil and blend well to form a purée. Scrape the mixture into a bowl and stir in the Parmesan. Taste and adjust the seasoning with salt and pepper. Set aside while you make the gnocchi.

Put the potatoes in a saucepan with cold salted water to cover. Bring to the boil and cook for 20–30 minutes, until soft. Drain well, let cool slightly, then peel. While still warm, pass through a potato ricer or mouli, or push through a sieve into a large bowl. Beat the flour into the potatoes, a little at a time. Stop adding flour when the mixture is smooth and slightly sticky. Season with salt to taste.

Turn out the mixture onto a well-floured board, then roll out the dough into long sausages about 1 cm in diameter. Cut each sausage into short pieces about 2 cm long. Put each piece on the end of your thumb and press the prongs of a fork lightly over the top. The pieces will be hollow on one side and grooved on the other. Put them on to a floured plate as you make them.

Bring a large saucepan of water to the boil. Add 20–25 pieces of gnocchi to the pan at a time. They will quickly rise to the surface. Cook for 10–15 seconds more, then remove with a slotted spoon and put in a bowl while you cook the rest. Add the pesto to the bowl and gently turn the gnocchi in the mixture until they are well coated. Serve immediately, sprinkled with extra Parmesan.

750 g large floury potatoes
125 g plain flour, plus extra for rolling
sea salt, to taste

WALNUT AND ROCKET PESTO
50 g rocket leaves, roughly chopped
25 g chopped walnuts
2 garlic cloves
125 ml extra virgin olive oil
25 g freshly grated Parmesan cheese, plus extra to serve
sea salt and freshly ground black pepper

SERVES 4

Dhaal baht (rice and lentils) is a staple meal for millions of Indians and Nepalis. In this recipe, *aloo* (potatoes) are added to that traditional duo, and they are particularly good for absorbing the wonderful flavours

indian potato curry

WITH TOOR DHAAL (YELLOW LENTILS)

125 g yellow lentils

3 tablespoons oil

½ teaspoon mustard seeds

½ teaspoon fenugreek seeds

1 teaspoon grated fresh ginger

1 teaspoon crushed garlic

1 teaspoon chilli powder

1½ teaspoons ground coriander

½ teaspoon ground turmeric

4 tomatoes, skinned and chopped

600 ml water

1 teaspoon salt

750 g floury potatoes, cut into 2 cm chunks

sea salt and freshly ground black pepper

TO SERVE

2 tablespoons chopped fresh coriander, plus extra sprigs

½ teaspoon garam masala

basmati rice

SERVES 4

Wash the lentils well in several changes of water. Heat the oil in a large saucepan over low heat. Add the mustard and fenugreek seeds. When they begin to pop, stir in the ginger and garlic and fry for 30 seconds.

Add the chilli powder, ground coriander and turmeric and stir-fry for a further 30 seconds. Add the tomatoes and lentils, cover with 600 ml water, add the salt, then bring to the boil. Reduce the heat, cover and simmer for 20–30 minutes or until the lentils are just soft.

Add the potatoes and simmer over low heat for 10–15 minutes or until the potatoes are tender. Season with salt and pepper.

Serve sprinkled with chopped coriander, garam masala and sprigs of fresh coriander. Basmati rice makes a suitable accompaniment.

potato gratin

WITH HERBS, SPINACH AND CHEESE

1 garlic clove, crushed

15 g unsalted butter, melted

500 g trimmed fresh spinach

3 eggs, beaten

500 ml crème fraîche

125 g grated Gruyère cheese

50 g chopped fresh herbs, such as chives, parsley, chervil or sorrel

a pinch of freshly grated nutmeg

a pinch of cayenne pepper

1.25 kg large waxy potatoes, thinly sliced

sea salt and freshly ground black pepper

TO SERVE

salad leaves, such as shin joi, red chicory (endive) or red shiso

vinaigrette dressing

sea salt

cracked black pepper

a springform cake tin, 23 cm diameter

SERVES 6–8

Mix the garlic and melted butter together and use to grease the springform cake tin.

Wash the spinach and put in a large saucepan with just the water that is left clinging to the leaves. Cover and cook, stirring once, until the spinach has just wilted. Drain well and squeeze out any excess moisture. Chop finely.

Beat the eggs with the crème fraîche, stir in the chopped cooked spinach and two-thirds of the Gruyère. Add the herbs and season well with nutmeg, cayenne, salt and pepper.

Cover the base of the cake tin with a layer of sliced potato and cover evenly with a spoonful of the cream and spinach mixture. Continue the layers, finishing with a layer of potato. Sprinkle with the remaining Gruyère, then cover the tin with foil.

Stand the cake tin in a roasting tin and pour enough boiling water around the cake tin to come half way up the sides. Carefully put in a preheated oven and cook at 180°C (350°F) Gas 4 for about 1½ hours or until the potatoes are tender – test by piercing the centre with a knife or skewer. Remove the foil for the last 15 minutes to let the top brown.

Turn out on to a plate and serve hot or cold, seasoned with salt and lots of cracked black pepper and with salad leaves sprinkled with vinaigrette dressing.

A wonderful creamy gratin of waxy potatoes layered with spinach, herbs, Gruyère and crème fraîche. It can be served hot or cold and would make an easily transportable picnic dish.

This soufflé of hot fluffy potato with nuggets of mozzarella and Fontina cheese melting through is the perfect comfort food.

potato soufflé

WITH MOZZARELLA AND ALMOND-PARSLEY PESTO

100 g unsalted butter (50 g melted, 50 g at room temperature)

50 g dry breadcrumbs

1.5 kg floury potatoes, unpeeled

150 ml milk, warmed

2 eggs, plus 1 egg yolk, beaten

50 g freshly grated Parmesan cheese

1 mozzarella cheese, about 125 g, drained and cut into cubes

125 g Fontina or Emmental cheese, cut into cubes

sea salt and freshly ground black pepper

rocket leaves, to serve

ALMOND-PARSLEY PESTO

1 bunch of fresh flat leaf parsley, washed and stalks removed

50 g almonds (with brown skins left on), toasted in the oven until golden, then cooled

250 ml extra virgin olive oil

75 g Parmesan cheese, grated

sea salt and freshly ground black pepper

a soufflé dish or cake tin, 23 cm diameter

SERVES 4

To make the pesto, grind the parsley, toasted almonds and 2 tablespoons olive oil to a rough texture using a mortar and pestle or a food processor. Scrape into a bowl, then stir in the remaining oil and Parmesan. Season to taste with salt and pepper

Grease the soufflé dish or cake tin well with half the melted butter, then coat well with half the breadcrumbs, shaking out any excess.

Put the potatoes in a large saucepan of lightly salted water and bring to the boil. Simmer for 20–30 minutes or until tender. Drain well and when cool enough to handle, peel and pass through a potato ricer or mouli, or push through a sieve into a large bowl. Add the butter at room temperature and warm milk and mix well. Add the beaten eggs, grated Parmesan and season well with salt and pepper. Mix well.

Spoon half the potato mixture into the prepared soufflé dish or cake tin, pushing it up against the sides with the back of the spoon. Sprinkle the cheese cubes over the top, then cover with the remaining potato mixture. Brush the top with the remaining melted butter and sprinkle with the remaining breadcrumbs.

Cook in a preheated oven at 180°C (350°F) Gas 4 for 20 minutes, then increase the temperature to 220°C (425°F) Gas 7 and cook for a further 10 minutes until the top is golden.

Sprinkle with the pesto and serve with a handful of rocket leaves.

accompaniments

This method of cracking the potatoes and cooking them in wine comes from Cyprus. Cooked slowly with coriander seeds, the potatoes absorb all the delicious juices.

cracked new potatoes

IN CORIANDER AND RED WINE

1 kg small new potatoes, unpeeled, scrubbed and dried

4 tablespoons olive oil

1 tablespoon coriander seeds, crushed

150 ml red wine

4 tablespoons chopped fresh coriander leaves

sea salt and freshly ground black pepper

SERVES 4–6

Put the potatoes in a clean tea towel and, using a wooden mallet or other heavy kitchen implement, thump the potatoes to crack them open. (Don't be over-zealous or you will end up with raw mashed potato!)

Heat the oil gently in a saucepan large enough to hold the potatoes in a single layer. Add the potatoes, coriander seeds, salt and pepper and cook, turning the potatoes occasionally until lightly golden all over.

Add the wine, let it boil, then reduce the heat. Cover the pan and simmer gently, shaking the pan occasionally, for 15–20 minutes or until the potatoes are tender.

Remove the pan from the heat and stir in the chopped coriander leaves. Serve as an accompaniment to meat or poultry.

champ

Put the potatoes in a large saucepan of lightly salted water and bring to the boil. Simmer for 20–30 minutes or until tender. Drain well. Meanwhile, put the spring onions in a saucepan with the milk, bring to the boil, then simmer for 2–3 minutes. Remove from the heat and let infuse for 10 minutes.

Press the potatoes through a potato ricer or mouli, or pass through a sieve into a large bowl. Beat in the milk and spring onion mixture, then beat in the butter, salt and pepper. Transfer to a clean saucepan and reheat gently. To serve, spoon into small bowls in mounds, make a hollow in the top and insert more butter and blue cheese, if using.

VARIATIONS

COLCANNON (SHOWN ABOVE LEFT), IRELAND
Kale, cabbage or another leafy green vegetable is used instead of the spring onion and cheese. It is served in the same way as champ, or formed into little cakes and fried in butter to form a crunchy crust.

CLAPSHOT, SCOTLAND
Follow the recipe for champ. Omit the cheese and add 750 g mashed swedes. Chives or bacon fat may also be added. The chopped spring onions are optional.

KAILKENNY, SCOTTISH HIGHLANDS
Follow the recipe for colcannon, adding 125 ml cream.

RUMBLEDETHUMPS, SCOTTISH BORDERS
750 g each of cooked potatoes and cabbage are thumped (mashed) then rumbled (mixed) with black pepper and 125 g butter. It is then topped with cheese and grilled until brown.

750 g floury potatoes, cut into even-sized pieces

a bunch of spring onions, including the green tops, chopped

300 ml milk

50 g butter, plus extra for serving

175 g blue cheese, crumbled (optional)

sea salt and freshly ground black pepper

SERVES 4

Champ is pure comfort food. Dip each forkful of potato in the little pool of butter before eating. Blue cheese, in this case Irish Cashel Blue, is my own optional addition!

This is perhaps the best-known of all Swedish potato recipes. The original uses butter and breadcrumbs, and sometimes Parmesan cheese is added.

bay-roasted hasselbacks

24 small potatoes, unpeeled and scrubbed

approximately 20 fresh bay leaves, torn in half lengthways

15 g unsalted butter

3 tablespoons olive oil

1–2 garlic cloves, crushed

sea salt flakes and freshly ground black pepper

SERVES 4–6

To prepare the potatoes, put 2 chopsticks side by side on a board and put a potato lengthways between them. Using a sharp knife, and holding the chopsticks and potato in place, make crossways cuts 3 mm apart, cutting just down to the sticks. Alternatively, spear each potato lengthways with a skewer about 5 mm from the base, slice across the potato as far as the skewer, then remove the skewer.

Insert a couple of pieces of bay leaf, or a whole leaf if small, in each sliced potato. Melt the butter with the olive oil in a heavy-based roasting tin over moderate heat. Stir in the garlic and gently add the potatoes in a single layer – take care, or the oil may splutter. Move them around for 2–3 minutes to colour slightly, then season with sea salt flakes and black pepper.

Put the tin in a preheated oven at 190°C (375°F) Gas 5 and roast for 25–30 minutes until golden brown and tender. As they cook, the potatoes will open out like a fan.

Serve as an accompaniment to meat or poultry, or to baked or roasted fish.

This traditional French cooking method has been enthusiastically adopted by modern American chefs. Cooking in a parcel means that the flavour and goodness of the potatoes is retained as they cook in their own steam. Let your guests open the parcels at the table.

potatoes en papillote

SCENTED WITH FRESH HERBS

500 g very small new potatoes, unpeeled and scrubbed

50 g unsalted butter

4 sprigs of fresh herbs such as thyme, tarragon, chervil, mint or rosemary

1 egg, beaten

sea salt

a baking sheet

greaseproof paper

SERVES 4

Cut out 4 sheets of greaseproof or parchment paper, 30 x 38 cm each, and fold in half lengthways. Draw a large curve in the shape of half a heart. Cut along the line and open out.

Put a quarter of the potatoes on one half of each piece of paper. Dot the butter evenly all over, sprinkle with sea salt and add a herb sprig to each one.

Brush the edges of the paper lightly with the beaten egg and fold over. Starting from the rounded end, pleat the edges together so that each parcel is completely sealed. Twist the ends together.

Put the parcels on a baking sheet and cook in a preheated oven at 200°C (400°F) Gas 6 for 25–30 minutes until the parcels are well puffed and the potatoes are tender. Serve immediately.

swiss rösti

Put the whole potatoes in a large saucepan and cover with cold water. Bring to the boil and cook for 10–15 minutes until the potatoes are just tender. Drain well, let cool slightly, peel, then grate coarsely into a large bowl.

Heat 2 tablespoons of the clarified butter in a frying pan, add the onion and bacon and cook for 5–6 minutes until the onions are softened. Add this mixture to the bowl of potato, season with salt and pepper and mix well.

1 kg potatoes, unpeeled and scrubbed

175 g clarified butter*

1 onion, chopped

125 g pancetta or streaky bacon, cut into thin strips

500 g wild or flat field mushrooms, or a mixture of both, cut in halves or quarters if large

2 tablespoons chopped fresh flat leaf parsley

sea salt and freshly ground black pepper

*To clarify butter, melt over gentle heat, then let cool. Skim off the pure butter and discard the solids and water.

SERVES 4

Heat half the remaining butter in a frying pan, add the potato mixture and press down slightly to form a large pancake. Cook for 10 minutes, adding a little extra butter around the edges and shaking the pan occasionally.

Cover the frying pan with a plate and carefully flip the pancake over. Add more butter to the frying pan, then slide the rösti back in to cook the other side. Add more butter around the edges of the rösti and cook until lightly golden, about 7 minutes. Remove from the heat and keep it warm.

Heat the remaining butter in a frying pan. Add the mushrooms and cook, stirring occasionally, for 3–5 minutes until tender but still firm. Season with salt and pepper, then stir in the parsley.

Serve the rösti topped with the mushrooms. An alternative option is to divide the rösti mixture into 4 parts before cooking to serve as a starter – or vary the topping according to taste, and serve with a few peppery salad leaves, like rocket.

These pancakes can also be served topped with Gruyère cheese, fried eggs, or served separately with meat and sausages.

Two of the finest French potato dishes are *gratin dauphinois* and *pommes à la dauphinoise*. They are very similar, but in the latter, sliced potatoes are baked with cream and garlic. To make *gratin dauphinois* a mixture of eggs, milk and cream is poured over the potatoes, they are then topped with cheese before baking.

pommes à la dauphinoise

Bring a small saucepan of water to the boil. Add the garlic, reduce the heat and simmer for 20 minutes until very tender. Remove the garlic, then crush well to a purée using a mortar and pestle, or press through a fine sieve.

4 garlic cloves

200 ml milk

450 ml double cream

1 kg floury potatoes, sliced into 5 mm slices

sea salt and freshly ground white pepper

a roasting tin or baking dish, about 25 x 15 cm, or a round cake tin, 23 cm diameter, greased

SERVES 4

Put the puréed garlic in a saucepan with the milk and cream, season well with salt and pepper, bring to the boil, then remove from the heat.

Arrange the potato slices in the greased roasting tin, dish or cake tin in 6 or 7 layers.

Pour over the cream mixture and press the potatoes down. The cream should come to just below the top layer. Cook in a preheated oven at 170°C (325°F) Gas 3 for 1½–2 hours, pressing the potatoes down gently every 20 minutes.

The cream will be absorbed gradually and the potatoes will become compressed and more solid as they cook. If there appears to be too much liquid, remove some with a spoon. When the top is coloured, stop pressing.

Test with a knife to check that the potatoes are cooked. Remove from the oven and let rest in a warm place for 10 minutes. Spoon straight from the dish or cut out shapes with pastry cutters for a more elegant serving.

baking

golden potato scones

WITH PARMESAN AND PANCETTA

4 slices of pancetta or bacon, about 50 g, cut into small pieces

150–175 g plain flour

2 teaspoons baking powder

½ teaspoon salt

50 g unsalted butter, cut into cubes, plus extra for serving

125 g cooked mashed potato

50 g Parmesan cheese, cut into tiny cubes

1 teaspoon dried oregano

about 2 tablespoons milk

1 egg yolk, beaten, to glaze

a fluted cutter, 6 cm diameter
a baking sheet, well greased

MAKES 10

Heat a frying pan without oil and dry-fry the pancetta or bacon for 5–6 minutes or until crispy. Remove with a slotted spoon and drain on kitchen paper.

Sieve the flour, baking powder and salt together into a large bowl. Add the butter and rub in using your fingertips until the mixture resembles breadcrumbs.

Add the potato, Parmesan, oregano and cooked pancetta or bacon pieces and mix well. Add enough milk to form a soft but firm dough. Turn out on to a lightly floured surface and knead briefly. Roll out the dough to 1.5 cm thick, then stamp out rounds using the fluted cutter. Re-roll any trimmings and cut more rounds, to make about 10 scones in total.

Put the scones on the well-greased baking sheet and brush the tops with the beaten egg. Cook in a preheated oven at 220°C. (425°F) Gas 7 for 10–15 minutes or until golden brown and well risen. Transfer to a wire rack and let cool a little. Serve while still warm, spread with unsalted butter.

honey potato bread

WITH SAFFRON AND A POPPYSEED GLAZE

250 g floury potatoes, cut
into even-sized pieces

a large pinch of saffron strands

425 g bread flour

1 teaspoon salt

1½ teaspoons easy-blend dried yeast

2 tablespoons honey

75 g unsalted butter, melted

2 egg yolks, beaten

125 g raisins

POPPYSEED GLAZE

1 egg white, beaten

1 tablespoon black poppyseeds

2 baking sheets, greased

MAKES 2 LOAVES

Put the potatoes in a large saucepan of lightly salted water and bring to the boil. Simmer for 20–30 minutes or until tender. Drain, reserving 250 ml of the cooking liquid in a bowl. Add the saffron strands to the reserved liquid and let steep for 30 minutes.

Pass the cooked potatoes through a potato ricer, mouli or push through a fine sieve into a large bowl. Add the reserved potato water and saffron and mix well.

Sieve the flour and salt into a large bowl and stir in the dried yeast. Add the potato mixture, honey, butter, egg yolks and raisins. Mix well to form a soft but firm dough. Turn out the dough on to a lightly floured surface and knead for 10 minutes. Put in an oiled bowl, cover and leave in a warm place for about 1–1½ hours or until doubled in size.

Turn out the dough on to a lightly floured surface, punch down and knead for a further 5 minutes. Cut in half and form into 2 round loaves. Put 1 loaf on each greased baking sheet and score each one with a knife in a criss-cross pattern. Cover loosely and let rise again for 45 minutes to 1 hour, until doubled in size once more.

Brush the tops of the loaves with egg white and sprinkle with poppyseeds. Cook in a preheated oven at 200°C (400°F) Gas 6 for 40 minutes or until the bottom sounds hollow when tapped. Let cool on a wire rack. Eat within 5 days or freeze for up to 1 month.

An updated version of an old-fashioned bread. Potato and potato flour produce bread with a moist texture that keeps well and is very good toasted.

index